SOUNDBITES

Groups, Bands, & Orchestras

Roger Thomas

Heinemann Library
Chicago, Illinois

GG RH

© 2002 Reed Educational & Professional Publishing
Published by Heinemann Library,
an imprint of Reed Educational & Professional Publishing,
Chicago, Illinois

Customer Service 888-454-2279

Visit our website at www.heinemannlibrary.com

Designed by Paul Davies and Associates
Originated by Ambassador Litho Ltd.
Printed at Wing King Tong in Hong Kong

06 05 04 03 02
10 9 8 7 6 5 4 3 2 1

Library of Congress Cataloging-in-Publication Data
Thomas, Roger, 1956-
  Groups, Bands, & Orchestras / Roger Thomas.
      p. cm. -- (Soundbites)
Includes bibliographical references (p.   ) and index.
  ISBN 1-58810-264-5
  1. Musical groups--Juvenile literature. [1. Musical groups.] I.
Title. II. Series.
  ML3928 .T46 2001
  784--dc21
                                    2001001724

Acknowledgments
The author and publishers are grateful to the following for permission to reproduce copyright material:
Cover photograph: Steve Gillett/Redferns.
pp. 4, 7, 8, 18, 20, 23 Lebrecht Picture Library; p. 5 Panos Pictures; pp. 6, 9, 11, 12, 13, 14, 17, 21, 22, 27 Redferns; pp. 10, 26 Corbis; p. 15 Retna; p. 16 Christian Him; p. 19 Photodisc; p. 24 Hulton Getty; p. 25 Sally Greenhill; p. 28 GetMusic.com; p. 29 Echo City.

Special thanks to John Ranck, D.M.A. for his comments in the preparation of this book.

Every effort has been made to contact copyright holders of any material reproduced in this book. Any omissions will be rectified in subsequent printings if notice is given to the publisher.

Some words are shown in bold, **like this.** You can find out what they mean by looking in the glossary.

Contents

Introduction

People have been gathering together to make music for as long as history has been recorded and probably for much longer than that. Unlike many other activities, such as eating and sleeping, music does not at first appear essential to human life. However, it is impossible to escape the basic elements that make up music: **pitch, dynamics, timbre,** and **rhythm.** We experience all these in the sounds of everyday life.

Where does music come from?

Our basic understanding of music comes from the ways in which we process important information about the world around us. Most natural sounds have a clear pitch that we use to gain information about the sounds themselves. For example, when we hear a dog bark, we know that if the bark is high-pitched, the dog is probably a small one, while a low-pitched bark more likely indicates a big dog. The timbre of a sound, or the mixture of elements that make a sound recognizable, can tell us even more—it allows us to tell the difference between the sound of glass breaking and the sound of a china plate breaking. Rhythm, too, has always played a crucial role in human life. Our understanding of rhythm tells us if someone's heart rate and breathing are regular and helps us to walk and run effectively, to chew our food safely, and to do physical work efficiently. Imagine trying to knock on a door without using a rhythm of some kind.

Today's music making developed from early human survival skills. People used their ability to interpret sounds to help with hunting and with avoiding predators.

These Aboriginal Australians are using sticks that are pounded on the ground. This kind of group percussion playing is thousands of years old and evolved from making loud noises to frighten away predators.

Music in prehistory

All these kinds of information were essential for the survival and development of human beings during **prehistoric** times. A high-pitched animal cry could indicate a small animal that could be hunted for food, and a low-pitched cry could mean a larger animal, possibly a dangerous predator to be avoided. The loudness of the sound helped show how close the animal was. The simple sound of raindrops could mean there would soon be pools of fresh drinking water, while the complex timbres of a thunderstorm pointed to possible danger. The irregular breathing of an animal wounded by a hunter showed that it was becoming weak and would soon provide fresh food. This ability to recognize and understand sounds eventually developed into music.

From life into art

Literature began with factual record keeping, and the visual arts began with cave paintings that preserved actual events, such as hunting. Music also developed from a set of practical skills. Early occupations like hunting, gathering food, and securing protection from predators often worked better when done in groups—so the music that evolved from these activities also likely developed as a group activity.

5

The First Musical Groups

We tend to see musicians making music on their own and groups of musicians as very different. However, all music, whether a public **solo** performance, a **melody** produced on a home computer, or even a baby playing with a rattle, involves many people. For example, a single cellist playing an unaccompanied piece of music may not be a "group" in the usual sense. However, he or she relies on the composer who wrote the music; the publisher that printed the music; the teachers who taught him or her how to listen to music, how to read a **score,** and how to play the instrument; the instrument maker who made the instrument (not to mention the instrument's original inventor), and so on. Then there are the

people who taught others how to build cellos, compose, and teach, and the people who taught them, as well as the influence of all the other musicians that those involved may have listened to, learned from, or been associated with. All music is the result of the efforts of a large number of people. A solo performer is perhaps best thought of as the single playing member of the "group" described above, a group that may extend all over the world and throughout history.

Making music together

The first human beings used their voices and the objects around them to make sounds, making them all "performers" in a sense.

A solo musician is really part of a much larger group—a group of all the different people involved, from the inventor of the instrument, to the composer, to the person who taught the musician to play.

It is likely that the earliest music making began in **prehistoric** times as a group activity, for the same reason people started doing other things in groups: it worked better. Hunting was easier when several hunters were involved, food gathering was more thorough when a whole group searched in a single area at once, and so on. It would have been more effective when a whole group of hunters used their voices and other noises to chase prey or to frighten away predators. As true music began to develop, the power of several voices, or of early **percussionists** using branches and rocks, when compared to the efforts of a single person, would probably have been clear. It is also likely that the earliest group music involved some form of worship celebration. This idea is still with us today, in music at religious gatherings, songs for special occasions (such as your friends singing "Happy Birthday" to you), and even football chants.

Formal music

Some of the earliest formal group music that we know existed is shown on carvings from the ancient Sumerian civilization, dating from around 3000 B.C.E. We know that music was seen as important in this society, because the musicians are shown playing for a royal official and because this picture was found on an artifact from the Sumerian city of Ur.

This ancient Sumerian artifact is one of the earliest known illustrations of group music making.

Orchestras

It is reasonable to assume that the idea of organized groups of musicians is as old as music itself. People were making music in groups well before the invention of instruments that were built for the purpose of playing music. In the **Western** world, the term "orchestra" has come to mean a large group of musicians playing a variety of instruments.

Early orchestras

The orchestra as we now know it did not evolve for purely musical reasons. The word itself comes from the Greek word *orkhestra*, meaning a space in front of a theater stage, such as that used by some singers and dancers involved in a play. When **opera** first began in Europe during the early seventeenth century, the singers were accompanied by small groups of musicians. As composers realized that the music could also be used to help describe the thoughts and emotions of the characters onstage, orchestras began to include more and more instruments with identical or similar instruments being grouped into sections. This change happened about the same time as the invention of the violin, an instrument that was well-suited to this new kind of large musical group. It had a louder and clearer sound than its predecessor, the viol. The Italian composer Claudio Monteverdi (1567–1643) had an orchestra that was made up largely of stringed instruments of various sizes, together with a harp. It probably included some other instruments as well. This grouping was regarded as the standard at the time.

Today's orchestras are generally led by a conductor, who directs the music and keeps time with a baton. However, this role only really developed in the early nineteenth century.

This gamelan orchestra is from Indonesia.

Further developments

By the mid-seventeenth century, French court composer Jean Baptiste Lully (1632–87) introduced woodwinds to his orchestra. However, it was not until the beginning of the eighteenth century that brass instruments began to be used regularly in orchestras. Even then, because communication between various countries was much slower than it is today, ideas about which instruments should be included varied from place to place. During the nineteenth century, improved instrument-making skills contributed to the production of many redesigned brass and woodwind instruments that would stay **in tune** and that could be played in different **keys.** These new developments also led to the orchestral music of the time becoming much more sophisticated.

The orchestra today

The modern Western orchestra is very similar to that of the nineteenth century, with a range of instruments that enable the group to play music from several centuries. A typical orchestra includes violins (usually in two sections), violas, cellos, double **basses,** flutes, clarinets, oboes, bassoons, horns, trumpets, trombones, a tuba, **timpani,** and other percussion. There are smaller chamber orchestras as well, often consisting only of violins, violas, cellos, and basses. The term "orchestra" is also used to describe large musical **ensembles** in other cultures, such as the gamelan orchestras of Bali and Java.

9

Chamber Groups and Small Instrumental Ensembles

Chamber music

"Chamber" is an old word for room, so "chamber music" simply means music that can be played in an ordinary room rather than in a concert hall. Today, the term is usually used to describe any instrumental music written for a group that is smaller than a full-scale orchestra. Chamber **ensembles** can combine many different instruments. Here are just a few examples:

- The string quartet is one of the best-known types of chamber groups. It consists of two violins, a viola, and a cello. A great deal of music is written for this very popular type of group.
- The string trio consists of two violins and a cello (or occasionally a violin, a viola, and a cello). It is traditionally seen as difficult to write music for the string trio because there is usually no viola to play the middle notes between the violin and cello parts.
- The piano trio is usually made up of a violin, a cello, and a piano or other keyboard instrument, often a harpsichord. This is a versatile grouping with a wide **repertoire.**

This string quartet is made up of two violins, a viola, and a cello.

Small classical groups are central to many other musical cultures, such as that of India, where great emphasis is placed on individual **virtuosity.**

- Wind ensembles come in many sizes and can include a wide variety of different woodwind instruments. The French horn is often the only brass instrument included, because its **muted,** gentle **tone** blends well with woodwind instruments, such as the flute and clarinet.
- The saxophone quartet consists of a **soprano, alto, tenor,** and **baritone** saxophone. The saxophone quartet is found both in classical music and **contemporary** jazz.
- The sonata is generally more a musical form than a type of group. However, it usually refers specifically to a **composition** for one string or wind instrument plus a piano (or harpsichord in the case of some earlier sonatas). Sonatas written for the piano or other keyboard instruments are generally **solo** pieces.

Other chamber groups

There are many other types of chamber groups in classical music, often mixing a variety of instruments. There is even a rough equivalent to chamber music within jazz. Clarinetist Jimmy Guiffre led a group consisting of clarinet, piano, and double bass, playing a reflective, highly structured form of music that became referred to as chamber jazz.

Choirs and Vocal Groups

Singing is one of the oldest ways of making music, and it is without a doubt one of the earliest forms of organized music. It is also the only form of music making that does not need access to any technology—even the simplest musical instruments need some kind of tool to make them.

The gospel choir is one of the musical traditions that have grown out of religious worship.

Different vocal ranges

Within any **vocal** group, the singers are usually divided into different singing parts according to the **pitch** and **range** of their voices. In a **Western** choir, these voices are (from highest to lowest): **soprano,** usually female, although there are also boy sopranos; **treble,** usually boys; **contralto,** female; **alto,** female; **tenor,** male; **baritone,** male; and **bass,** male. There is also another male voice called countertenor, an artificially high voice used in some early vocal music.

Singing and worship

Singing has always been an important part of religious worship, and many pieces of music have been written for this purpose. Group singing multiplies the power of a single voice many times, adding strength to the message of the worshipers.

Many forms of worship have **choral** traditions. Early Christian vocal music was called plainchant, because it was a very simple, unornamented style (plain) with no instrumental accompaniment (chant). It was believed that if the music was complex and instruments were used, this would take away from the seriousness of the act of worship. In other cultures, including Native American, Aboriginal Australian, and Hindu, it is also felt that music in religious ceremonies should be simple and direct.

The vocal tradition in the Christian church now usually includes group singing on two levels: the trained group of singers in the choir that leads the singing, joined by a much larger group in the congregation whose abilities vary.

Cross-cultural choirs

Perhaps because singing is such a universal activity, there is a great deal of interest in the choral traditions of different cultures. One example, Zulu choral music, combines **close harmonies** with African **rhythms.** Another example is the unusual Bulgarian choral tradition that developed with a particular emphasis on women's voices—due to the fact that the male population of the country was often away at war.

Community choirs

In many countries throughout the world, there is a tradition of amateur choirs whose members come from from the local area. These are both a rich source of music making and a social focus for the members. This tradition extends into other vocal forms, from **opera** to barbershop singing. Choirs may also be associated with particular orchestras.

Barbershop vocal groups perform popular songs in arrangements using close harmonies.

Rock Bands

These days it is possible to find rock bands playing at every level of performance, from teenagers' garage bands to massive stadium concerts. However, during its early history, playing rock music to any high standard was often an impossible dream for many who could not find or afford the specialized instruments this style required.

Instrumentation was very basic in early rock and roll.

The roots of rock instrumentation

Rock music developed from a variety of popular American musical **genres,** including country music, dance band music, jazz, and blues. Most of the types of music that preceded rock were relatively undemanding in terms of the instruments they required—usually inexpensive guitars, fiddles, harmonicas, and brass instruments that could often be bought cheaply. This tradition has been preserved in various forms of American folk music. The only percussion instrument in Cajun music, for example, is a triangle.

The invention of **amplified** guitars and **bass** guitars was originally intended to make these instruments easier to hear in dance bands. However, it soon became clear that this adaptation allowed a much smaller group to perform to a large audience. Just as important, it allowed the players to use the characteristics of amplified sound to give rock music a special feel. The drum set had already developed from a collection of assorted percussion instruments used in the theater into a sophisticated combination of instruments assembled for a specific purpose. The recording and broadcasting industries were progressing during the same period, making the marriage of rock music and technology inevitable.

Rock instruments today

For the first generation of rock musicians, quality instruments were few in number and very expensive. Today, instrument technology is both far better and far cheaper. The core of a modern rock band will usually include:

- one or more guitarists, who generally use electric instruments played through amplifiers;
- a bassist, typically playing an electric bass guitar through an amplifier; and
- a drummer, playing a specifically assembled set consisting of snare and bass drums, cymbals, and snareless **semi-pitched drums** called tom-toms, or just toms.

Many bands also have a keyboard player. Today, in addition to the piano or the electronic organ, there is a wide variety of sophisticated electronic keyboards available.

Singing may involve a lead singer and possibly backup singers as well. They use microphones and a large amplification system called a PA (public address) system.

A horn section of saxophones and brass instruments, a **percussionist,** and a **DJ** (who can add sounds from vinyl records) may also be involved.

Electric guitars back up Lenny Kravitz during a performance. The whole performance is amplified.

Jazz Groups

Jazz music has developed continuously since its beginnings early in the twentieth century. The main instruments used in this musical style originated with those used in military and marching bands. Today, most instruments in existence have been put to use in the performance of jazz music at one time or another—including, in the case of one musician named Rufus Harley, the bagpipes! However, there are some instruments that are much more common in jazz today than others.

The main instruments of a jazz group

Supporting the music of a typical jazz group from every period, the **rhythm** section traditionally consists of piano, drums, and double **bass** or bass guitar. The section is so named to distinguish it from the "front line" of **melody** instruments. A guitar may be used as part of the rhythm section in larger bands or as a front-line instrument in smaller groups.

Reed instruments, including the various sizes of saxophones and clarinets, are among the most important instruments in a jazz group, because they tend to play most of the main themes and melodies.

Brass instruments, especially the trumpet and trombone (and occasionally the gentler-**toned** flügelhorn), were actually used in jazz before the saxophone and are still just as important.

A typical jazz quartet consists of a saxophone, electric guitar, bass guitar, and drum set.

Instrumental innovations in jazz

Jazz is a musical **genre** founded on experimentation, so jazz musicians are always looking for new instrumental ideas—using new instruments and sometimes even playing them in new and different ways. For example, electronic keyboards of various kinds are now well-established in jazz. These were preceded by the electronic organ and the electric piano, both of which are electromechanical (part electronic, part mechanical) instruments. Modern **digital** keyboards offer an even wider variety of sounds.

Innovative **contemporary** jazz orchestras can include all sorts of combinations of instruments.

Other stringed instruments, even the harp, are occasionally used in jazz. One of the most commonly used, the violin, was central to early **acoustic swing** music and is often used in modern jazz with **amplification.**

Other brass instruments, including the tuba, the French horn, and typical marching band instruments such as the **tenor** horn are sometimes included in jazz arrangements. The sousaphone, a very large type of bass tuba, was often used as the bass instrument in early jazz.

Tuned percussion is found in jazz in the form of the vibraphone. It consists of tuned metal bars with **tube resonators** underneath, with small motorized fans above the resonators and below the bars to add a gentle **tremolo** to the vibraphone's sound.

Latin percussion, consisting of **congas, bongos, timbales, cowbells, wood blocks,** and many hand percussion instruments, is widely used in both Latin-based jazz and in other forms of music.

17

Military and Marching Bands

The armed forces in most countries have military bands. These were originally used on the battlefield to provide signals that could be heard above the noise of the fighting. However, they developed into sophisticated musical units that are often used for ceremonies, parades, and public entertainment. Drums, brass, and woodwinds are the main instruments in these bands. Many instruments were originally invented or adapted for use in military bands. Ex-military musicians have brought their knowledge into **civilian** life, leading to the creation of marching bands in schools, colleges, and local communities. Like choirs, these bands are often an important social focus in community life.

The history of the modern marching band is strongly associated with the work of American composer and bandleader John Philip Sousa (1854–1932), whose expertise resulted in his band touring the world in 1910. Since then, many different instruments have been used in marching bands. These can include many woodwind instruments, such as the piccolo, flute, clarinet, **alto** and **tenor** saxophones, oboe, and bassoon.

The American marching band tradition is a thriving musical culture.

These bands also use the same types of brass instruments found in symphony orchestras, such as the trumpet, trombone, and French horn. In addition, there may be specialized brass instruments, many of which have been developed specifically for use in military and marching bands. These include the marching tuba (that is carried on the shoulder, unlike the orchestral tuba), the bugle (also still used as a signaling instrument), the cornet (a relative of the trumpet), the mellophone (shaped like a trumpet, but actually related to the French horn), and the euphonium (a type of small tuba).

An important element of all these groups are drums, including snare drums (often known by their original name of side drums, due to the position in which they are usually carried for marching), tenor drums, tom-toms (often in multiple sets), and **bass** drums (often several, with varied **pitches**). Other percussion can include cymbals, lyre bells (essentially a **glockenspiel** mounted on a lyre-shaped frame), and xylophones.

Different approaches

In the United Kingdom (U.K.), there are several interesting variations on the marching band. Scottish military bands, for instance, traditionally consist of drums and Highland bagpipes. More unusual in the early twentieth century are the marching **kazoo** bands that were popular in some parts of the U.K. as well as in the United States, where the instrument was invented in 1850. The musicians played simple kazoos, or "tommy talkers," that were often fitted with trumpetlike bells or were adapted by their owners to resemble traditional band instruments, such as trombones. Marching kazoo bands used to be referred to locally as "jazz bands," to the confusion of visiting jazz fans who would attend their performances expecting something quite different.

The kazoo is a very simple instrument to play.

Folk Groups

The usual definition of folk music is music that has its origins in popular culture, rather than being an art form produced by professional composers and musicians. However, sometimes there is no real distinction between folk music and art music. Some cultures see music as something to take part in rather than as a form of entertainment that musicians present to an audience. At the same time, there are many full-time, professional folk musicians who make music using many folk styles.

It is also hard to generalize about the instruments used in folk music worldwide, as these are determined by the instruments **indigenous** to each culture. However, there are some elements that are constant. The instruments used in folk music are usually relatively simple and readily available. For example, there is no folk music for the pipe organ, because it is a large instrument that is usually installed in a building. There is a great deal of folk music played on the violin (known as the fiddle in this musical style), because the instrument is portable and can be bought inexpensively. Despite the fact that both the violin and the cello share links with **Western** classical music, there is no tradition of playing folk music on the cello, presumably because it is larger and usually more expensive.

The fiddle and the **bodhran** are important in Irish folk music, such as that played by this traditional folk group from Ireland.

The Irish band The Corrs is an electric "folk-rock" group. Their music combines modern rock with more traditional folk sounds.

Folk instruments in the West

Instruments traditionally linked to folk groups in Western culture include the following:

- Fretted instruments, including the **acoustic** guitar, banjo, mandolin, mandola, and **bouzouki,** are among the most widely seen instruments in folk music today. They come from many different countries, showing how folk music is becoming increasingly international.
- Wind instruments, such as tin whistles and flutes, are important as well. There is also a strong tradition of folk bagpipes in many cultures.
- Percussion instruments, including typical examples like frame drums (such as the Irish bodhran) and rattling and clapping instruments (such as the bones—flat sticks of bone or wood that are clicked between the fingers), are often used.
- Homemade instruments are also found, such as a pair of spoons used as clappers or a bottle blown across the neck to make **bass** notes.
- Bellows instruments, such as the **concertina,** are found in the folk music of both Europe and the United States.
- The voice remains one of the most important elements of folk music. For many centuries, folk songs have served as an important form of popular entertainment and also as a way of communicating concerns. Folk songs often tell stories of love, war, humor, or imaginary events, but there are also many folk songs that express discontent—with a country's politics, for example.

Groups Around the World

Every culture has its own tradition of making music in groups, but the origins and traditions of these groups can differ widely. The following examples from various cultures across the world show this **diversity.**

- India: One example of Indian vocal music is *qawwali,* a tradition of songs that are often presented formally to audiences but that can cover very down-to-earth subjects, such as love and marriage. A *qawwali* group typically has a lead singer, a chorus of accompanying singers, and some instrumentalists.

- Scotland: The pipe band is frequently associated with Scottish music. Consisting of Highland bagpipes and drums, these bands are generally attached to military regiments and often give public performances during parades and other events.
- The Southern United States: The Cajun community is descended from a group of French-speaking settlers, so traditional Cajun songs are usually sung in French. The instruments typically used are fiddles, accordions, and triangles.
- Cuba: The Cuban **samba** tradition is nurtured by "samba schools," highly competitive trained bands that take part in parades and competitions. The bands use Latin percussion instruments as well as a variety of percussion instruments unique to this tradition. These

The bagpipes give a unique sound to Scottish pipe bands.

Steel bands are traditional West Indies bands that use tempered oil drums. These days the drums are usually specially made in a factory.

include the bomba (a deep-toned drum) and the tamborim and pandeiro (two types of frame drums).

- Russia: The balalaika is a traditional Russian instrument similar to a **lute,** but with a distinctive triangular body. There is even a tradition for assembling large balalaika orchestras using instruments of various sizes, including a **bass** instrument so large that it has to be rested on a spike.

- The West Indies, the U.K., and elsewhere: The steel band that originated in Trinidad has a unique and distinctive sound. The steel pans played by the musicians were originally made by **tempering** old oil drums. Today such instruments tend to be made in factories. A steel band uses several different types of pans, with various **pitch ranges.** The drums are named according to their sound, pitch, or function within the band: **rhythm** drums, ping-pong, second pan, cello, guitar, and bass drums.

These examples are only a few of the thousands of different musical groupings that exist in **Western** and non-Western cultures. The desire to make music in a group is common to all societies.

Informal Groups

While there are now any number of other sources of music, people of all ages still choose to make music in a group just for fun. The music usually takes the form of singing, and may enhance an already happy occasion or lift the spirits of the singers if they are in some sort of difficult situation. One memorable example of the latter occurred during the sinking of a ferry in the North Sea. Some of the survivors passed the time waiting to be rescued by singing a humorous song called "Always Look on the Bright Side of Life."

Fortunately, there are far more examples of spontaneous group singing that occur under more pleasant circumstances. One example is appropriately called a sing-along. A group of people join in singing, sometimes at home, while traveling (often in a car or bus), or in a public gathering place like a restaurant or park.

Children's songs and rhymes are usually learned at school, where older children pass them on to new generations of students. This is similar to the oral (spoken) tradition that exists in cultures where songs and stories are passed down verbally rather than being written down. These rhymes can have a wide range of themes, such as the common topic of love and marriage (for example, "Susie and Johnny

Slaves' work songs are an example of group singing under difficult or oppressive conditions.

Children's songs, games, and early education often involve group singing.

sitting in a tree, K-I-S-S-I-N-G"). Some others have historical origins, such as "Yankee Doodle," a song that was written during the American Revolution. Songs like this were written to encourage those fighting, state political opinions, and offer hope. In cultures where it is acceptable, children are also taught group singing at school.

Audience participation has a long history as a part of popular culture, and there are many forms of musical entertainment where the audience is encouraged to join in as a group. One example is the music hall tradition, a form of variety show popular in Victorian Britain that is similar to **vaudeville** in the United States. The audience is expected to know songs and choruses, which may be distributed on sheets of paper, and to join in as required. This also happens at rock concerts, where the audience is likely to sing along to songs they know and are often encouraged to do so by the performers. In this setting, participation is generally assumed to show the audience's support and enthusiasm, but if an audience were to do the same during an **opera,** it would indicate insensitivity and a lack of appreciation for the music.

Solo and Virtual Groups

As discussed earlier, even a single musician performing alone represents a whole group of people who have made the performance possible. Developments in technology, however, have made this into a much more direct process—a single musician can now make the kind of music normally associated with a group. But in a way, all these new possibilities have taken away some of the unique experience of making music in the company of other real human beings.

A "one-man band" combines the properties of a **solo** artist and group music.

Early developments

To be able to perform as a group, a musician must be able to artificially add to his or her abilities. One option is to use instruments that produce sound with little or no input by the musician. This is actually a very old idea—there are many types of "self-playing" instruments that date back to ancient times. Examples include the Aeolian harp, a stringed instrument that is placed outdoors so that the wind makes its strings **resonate;** wind chimes that are often used as domestic ornaments; and water chimes, a traditional Japanese instrument with a delicate sound made by water dripping onto thin, flat surfaces. It is likely that human beings' first experiments with sound made use of other natural phenomena as well, such as the echoes within a cave.

The poor sound quality of the first recorded music made it unsuitable for use in a performance situation or even for radio broadcasting. However, there was an earlier and quite successful means of replaying sound, specifically piano performances—the player piano. Its system allowed recordings to be made using a mechanism that would punch a hole in a roll of paper each time a note was played. This could then be played back by the instrument as it recognized the positions of the holes and played notes accordingly. Many famous musicians, including German composer Johannes Brahms (1833–97), made piano rolls. Other "low-tech" solutions include the one-man band (a single musician playing numerous instruments using straps, cables, and levers) and the cinema organ (that allows a range of sounds from real instruments, like cymbals and drums, to be played from a keyboard).

Technology and the virtual group

With the advent of modern instrumental technology, it has become possible for any single musician to perform group music. Some examples of this are:

- Auto-accompaniment, programming, and sequencing: Computers and keyboards can record several musical parts as **digital** data and replay them all together;
- Multitracked recordings: A single musician can record several instrumental parts separately and combine them to make a multi-instrument solo recording; and
- **DJ**-ing and remixing: A single DJ can create new pieces of music by mixing and remixing existing recordings.

A single DJ is able to create many different sounds at the same time, giving the illusion of a large group.

The Future of Group Music Making

From the time the very first groups made music together until now, one factor has remained constant—the obvious need for the people involved to cooperate and act together. Any group of people needs to be organized in order to produce effective music. However, modern music technology and communications media such as the Internet appear to have changed this somewhat.

Absentee musicians

While commercial recordings involving a number of musicians are presented as being the products of a concerted artistic effort on the part of all involved, this can often be a very false impression. The technology that allows each instrument and voice in a group to be recorded individually also provides opportunities to revise the music in different ways. It even allows individual parts to be recorded at different times and places. For example, if the members of a successful band all live in different countries, they do not need to gather in the same place to make their next hit record. They can record their parts separately and have an engineer and producer mix them. This means that it is possible for the members of a musical group to never meet each other.

In the 1980s, music technology changed with the widespread introduction of the compact disc. Today, you can download music directly from the Internet from websites like this one.

Sound sculptures

The U.K. group Echo City performs and creates "community sound sculptures," making a kind of "playground" full of **participatory** percussion instruments.

Impossibly perfect musicians

Digital editing can allow producers and engineers not just to correct a musical part, but also to change it entirely. So, any individual contribution to a group may end up sounding quite unlike what was originally intended.

No musicians

During the rise of disco in the 1980s, many opportunities for live music were lost, as venues were more willing to book **DJs.** Because DJs' contributions were based on recorded music, these performances were both simpler to stage and musically reliable. This shortage of opportunities caused many musicians to abandon live group music.

The new generation

Group music making has cleverly sidestepped these problems. The Internet has provided the perfect means for musicians to exchange information, with worldwide communication now being the norm. Community-based bands and orchestras are stronger than ever, and live group music flourishes in non-**Western** cultures. New types of live performance groups have arisen, mixing music with dance, theater, or community activities in ways that cannot be replaced by technology. It seems that the need to make music together will always be with us after all.

Glossary

acoustic referring to sound; also can describe an unamplified instrument

acoustic swing type of popular music, related to jazz, that features unamplified instruments

alto pitch range that is lower than soprano but higher than tenor

amplify to make louder

baritone low pitch range above bass but lower than tenor

bass lowest range of notes in general use

bodhran Irish folk drum

bongo small hand drum widely used in Latin and Afro-Cuban music, usually played as a pair

bouzouki Greek fretted and stringed instrument

choral performed by a group of singers

civilian not belonging to the armed forces

close harmony singing in which each voice sings a complementing melody close to the other voices

composition piece of written music

concertina handheld reed instrument operated by bellows

conga large hand drum used mainly in Latin and Afro-Cuban music

contemporary of the present day

contralto pitch range (and name for a singing voice) above alto and below treble

cowbell hollow metal percussion instrument played with a stick; widely used in Latin music but also in other musical forms

digital using a "language" of electronic ones and zeros

diversity wide variety of something

DJ performer who plays and mixes music from recordings; short for "disc jockey"

dynamics loudness or softness of a sound

ensemble small group of musicians

genre specific style, as with music or other art forms

glockenspiel percussion instrument consisting of tuned metal bars that are played with beaters

in tune producing notes that are accurate in pitch and that match those of any other instruments being played

indigenous native to a particular place

kazoo instrument that buzzes when a person hums or sings through it; usually a metal or plastic tube with a side hole covered by a thin membrane

key system of notes used in a piece of music, based on a chosen scale and named after the first note of that scale; for example, "the key of C"

lute round-backed fretted and stringed instrument that preceded the guitar

melody main tune in a piece of music

muted having a sound that is muffled or quieted

opera form of theatrical performance in which all the words are sung, usually to orchestral accompaniment

participatory allowing people to take part in, such as an activity

percussionist musician who plays percussion instruments

pitch highness or lowness of a note

prehistoric before history was formally recorded

range total number of notes an instrument or voice can reach, from the lowest to the highest

reed strip of cane that vibrates when air is blown across it

repertoire collection of musical pieces written for or performed by a person or group

resonate to vibrate in the presence of sound

rhythm time, pulse, and beat of music

samba Afro-Cuban form of music and dance

score musical composition, including all the instrumental and vocal parts, written down as sheet music

semi-pitched drum drum that can be tuned higher or lower but that does not have a clearly defined note

solo section or piece of music featuring a single performer with a group; one person performing alone is called a soloist

soprano pitch range higher than alto, contralto, and treble; the highest range in general use

temper to adjust the sound of an instrument by heating and hammering it during manufacture

tenor pitch range that is lower than alto but higher than baritone

timbale single-headed drum used in Afro-Cuban music; usually made of metal and played with thin sticks

timbre distinctive quality of a sound

timpani large single-headed drums with metal shells used mainly in classical music

tone quality of a sound

treble pitch range (and name for a singing voice) above contralto and below soprano

tremolo rapid variation in the loudness of a sound

tube resonator cylindrical tube found on some percussion instruments that makes the sound of the instrument louder

vaudeville onstage entertainment featuring a variety of music, comedy, and other acts

virtuosity exceptional musical ability

vocal having to do with the voice and singing

Western of or relating to North America and the countries of Europe

wood block percussion instrument made of wood, with a slot cut in it that acts as a resonator

Further Reading

Barber, Nicola (ed.). *The Kingfisher Young People's Book of Music.* New York: Larousse Kingfisher Chambers, 1999.

Dearling, Robert. *Keyboard Instruments & Ensembles: Encyclopedia of Musical Instruments.* Broomall, Penn.: Chelsea House Publishers, 2000.

Rowe, Julian. *Music.* Chicago: Heinemann Library, 1998.

Index